PRAISE FOR CRYSTAL STONE

"Crystal Stone's wickedly sharp imagination and masterful control of imagery left me shouting "wow" into an empty room over and over again. The poems in *All the Places I Wish I Died* offer warmth and comfort amidst terrible lonely, desire that outlives its beloved, and these poems ferry us through a hall filled with mirrors that each reflect the intimacy of human connection in a new way. Stone writes " Every disorder / is a form of coping—the tragedy / of being born into the poems we are". Stone opens the door to her world with these poems, and trusts us to step in willingly, knowing we won't want to turn back."

— BRANDON MELENDEZ, AUTHOR OF *GOLD THAT FRAMES THE MIRROR*

"Crystal Stone's *All the Places I Wish I Died* is truly teeming with life. It lives in a world of odes and autocorrect, beer and Sauvignon Blanc. These poems love and lose with a terrifying beauty, where "loneliness is not a rainbow, but a wandering strand." In this modern woman's lamentation, Stone is unafraid to admit the danger of love, "what it feels like to care for anything without losing the night." *All the Places I Wish Died* is a book "destined to hurt" where the heart needs it most."

R OF *UGLY MUSIC* AND **2020** WHITING AWARD WINNER

"In her stunning collection, *All the Places I Wish I Died*, Crystal Stone admits, "I write / poems about something I can't touch" before making the intangible—love, desire, loss—tangible. This book invites us to explore the depths of its speaker's past experiences—each poem becomes an exercise in l'esprit de l'escalier—only here, revisiting the past alters the present. And through this altering, Stone reveals a new kind of lonely--one where you lose yourself through your re/encounters with others—"After so much time touching other things, / my hands stopped tasting like me." Read *All the Places I Wish I Died* and pay close attention to the poems that leave their own taste in your mouth."

— PAIGE LEWIS, AUTHOR OF *STAR STRUCK*

"Crystal Stone's *All the Places I Wish I'd Died* is the friend on the line when we've called "the suicide hotline" and the volunteer asks if "there's a friend we could call" instead. These poems walk us around the house in a bathrobe carrying all the poems we've ever loved, all the voices that have saved us, and then searches the fridge with us anyway for something to eat, only to find "Goldilocks milk with lukewarm curdles." Unabashed, these poems admit, "I eat tomato soup with moldy basil / for breakfast because don't we all want / more green?" These poems understand; they take our hand and assure us, "Grief is a supervised visit / to the butterfly wing." Wry and ironic, yet tender and self-aware in a way that gets at communal awareness, at holding each other in the lines, Stone confides: "sometimes it's comforting / to know we're almost all suffering the same way." I love this book. I'll be carrying its keen observations and nuanced affirmations with me like worry stones."

— JENN GIVHAN, *GIRL WITH DEATH MASK* AND *ROSA'S EINSTEIN*, FORMER NEA FELLOW

ALL THE PLACES I WISH I DIED

CRYSTAL STONE

LEGEND

A man sits next to a woman, runs
his fingers—lightning—through

her hair. It shocks. She stabs
until his blood makes little

rubies she strings around her neck.
The table stained glass. She walks

to church and uses the gems
as a rosary. She does not pray for him.

She prays for sister, mother,
aunt. They lock the woman

away, steal her rubies.
No poetry written on the wall.

the poem begins not where the knife enters
but where the blade twists.

— Hanif Abdurraqib-Willis

I.

Killing yourself slowly is still killing yourself. Wanting to die
is not the same thing as wanting to come home. Recovery
is hard work.

— BLYTHE BAIRD

The attempt to eradicate oneself doesn't actually work. You stay
who you are.

— JENNIFER MICHAEL HECHT, FROM *STAY: A HISTORY OF
SUICIDE AND PHILOSOPHIES AGAINST IT*

TAKE IT FROM A RUFOUS-COLLARED SPARROW

after Linda Gregg

What knows to love? Not a mother
cowbird dropping her young into
another mother's nest. She watches
nearby for signs of abuse, but never
interferes until her child is murdered.
Most of the time, the chick eats.
Then grows. Eventually flies
to another's nest, still incapable
of affection. Like she knows she is
adopted, bigger than the rest, born
to bully. Now, she is older, feathers
thinning: two children come and gone,
orphaned and still she flies solo,
from one man to another. Always
traveling. Always following.
All of her children loners. All of her
offspring singing another bird's song.

AGAINST SENTIMENTALITY

I'm roller skating in the oldest
punk house in America, I'm told.
I want to believe it. We all want
to be the biggest, the best, the first.
Every poem answers a question
I'm still defining. At a stranger's house
before bed, the cats eat kibble with weed.
Autocorrect changes "hosts" to "ghosts."
I believe it. Every disorder
is a form of coping—the tragedy
of being born into the poems we are.
I leave on roads with high waters
in a rental car. The poem floods. So many
streets closed. A man tells me,
you broke down in the wrong town
& he doesn't just mean the car.
My car has a face I remember,
unlike the men I want to objectify
in conversations and short poems.
That's all I can take with me.

Wet kisses on dry days I think about
when I walk through the conservatory
with baby tears plants & petunia night
skys. I watch new men walk by
and I check out their asses.
I'll be happy to be home long enough
to masturbate without interruption, a man's
hairy stomach, vulgar words. To read
a book, *Ugly Music,* in the quiet glitter
of lightning in the newly black sky.

EVEN WHEN IT LOOKS LIKE EVERYTHING IS RIGHT, IT ISN'T

Oatmeal on the table with almond milk, peanut butter, and honey.

Oatmeal in the tub. Skin covered with ivy's lingering lipstick stain.

Oatmeal in the cupboard. Six-month old yogurt in the fridge.
He said, "Dairy doesn't really expire."

Crystals in the honey. Milk thrown up in chunks.

Expanding chia in the fridge. He said, "More beautiful, thicker."

Bacon, sliced. Undercooked in the pan & fatty.

Goldilocks milk with lukewarm curdles.

TO THE WOMAN WHO FEELS NO PAIN
DUE TO A GENETIC MUTATION

On the way to the airport, the taxi driver says
everyone should have a row of horns
so he knows exactly what each sound means.
He thinks horns are screaming babies, sounds
without language. He doesn't know what
they're saying. From his car, there's no way
to ask. The man next to me on the plane
listens to an audiobook on the Celtic holocaust.
I don't ask what he learns. I'm still high.
I know when we descend because a baby cries.
The baby has ears, too. They pop—horns.
The clouds are scattered cells. My genetic
mutations won't help anyone else.
A protruding bone on my foot's arch
and other hardnesses. Is it lonely to live
without pain? I've always wished my body could be
free, but sometimes it's comforting
to know we're almost all suffering the same way.

POEM WITH DEPRESSION

He said eat a cat or breakfast
He said bigger beautiful same thing
He said how dare you love isn't a reason
He said you stay
He said drink my tears I don't have any
He said I did it for you your love is broken
He said here's some gas money
He said here's a fig your vagina is tight
He said flowers
He said don't let them drown
He said there's darkness inside you it isn't me
He said I'll pay you to quit
He said five dollars less you won't kill the bees
He said I have guns in the house don't snoop
He said you will remember me but how
He said it's my house you just have a key
He said you're the bed I'm in
He said I'm not angry anymore
He said I'm losing are you
He said fewer questions it's hard to talk

He said you're using me I don't know how
He said to live love is pain
He said the shower is dirty
He said it didn't used to be this way
He said I taped it up the roaches came out
He said I know you're tired let's recess
He said here's some aspirin
He said no no that's too much
He said come on here's a drawer climb in

APRIL, IN THE GRASS

I am a linen of lightning   bugs   the bellflowers
        bride   my hair a veil I would not   otherwise
wear the bunnies   guillotine the marigolds   when
        they die   more bitter than bright   the flies
eat   its flesh & irises   but who loves
        azalea in spring   only purple when sun sycamores
the garden   even I have more grit   than them
        my lips indigo   in the freeze   does it scare you
that my dreamcatchers are too full for your nightmares
        if they flew   towards me   I would choke
on butterflies   velvet my tongue   with pollen
        but they don't notice   I'm here   mouth
open even with my arms   wide I'm no milkweed
        of limbs   I am the pollen   unhoneyed
I don't photosynthesize   in the rays I flame

TO THE WOMAN WHO SAID I WAS "TOO NORMAL" FOR THERAPY

I.

sleep is stale grass I lay in   no blanket   no silk

    my eyes swamp   their own mud dry,   moisten the ceiling fog

there are days I don't move   my stepmom told her friend

this place is so lonely   she only visited   me a few hours

no one stays here for long   I stopped asking   the public is too

heavy   to hold   my lungs would have teeth before they had a voice

II.

I stopped eating dinner   without salt   I don't make

music anymore,   I break strings.   The backs of crawfish.

Men I want buy me   more   or don't   I've stopped breathing

in my sleep if I make it there   he said I scared him some nights

but he wasn't ready   to run out of stories   even though he did

III.

run, I am the blank   at the book's beginning   I never end

them   but I am wide open   the unfinished zombies good

friends a memory   I admit that I don't recognize most

of the men I thought   I loved   I'm unfair   to the trees

I used   to write them off   when I'm so good at forgetting

and everywhere is   a place I feel I've never been.

PORTRAIT OF THE ALCOHOLIC'S DAUGHTER

I never know until it happens
    the day you understand the hollow

cello in my living room dusty
    candles on my dresser

clothes picked
    from others' discards I find love

the same way I try to imagine
    it's possible to build a house of straw

when it's all there is to use
    the gypsy moth can't think about shelter

her young birth parasitic flies and die
    my mother lit red candles on the floor

with faces of saints
    she didn't bring them

the day I saw my first ghost
    I was six walking through

the narrow motel hallway
    in the middle of nowhere

there was blood on the headboard mom
    told me to stop telling stories

my brother was silent
    nothing to say

when this happened
    not the first day I woke up

in the middle of a nightmare
    her screaming why

aren't you happy
    I've felt guilty ever since

my brother begs me to stop
    he loved her in a way I did not

until I read the poem she wrote about me
    ten years before I was born

she died seven years ago now
    in her bed next to a man she didn't love

but I sleep more soundly next to you
    than I ever have next to someone else

and prepare for the sun to argue
  with the moon

about what time it is
  always trying

to outshine the other
  chronically far apart

SELF PORTRAIT IN A THUNDERSTORM

Yellow skies and no storm sirens.
Hail bursts large enough to break
my window. I think about letting nature in
to clean my carpet. The thunder is
a heartbeat, mine. My eyes june
with longer days—they warm
and lengthen. The prairie grasses
outside look blue because my eyes
want them watering beaches
instead of streets. I want my bed
to boat my body on the coast I miss.
My hair is spring, blooms fly aways.
I've lost so much—many poems, always
listening to others. They tornado my mind
empty of my words. I don't want
to sound like the men I've talked to.
Only the women. Only the earth.
Only the grasses, wind, hail and sky.

GRASSHOPPER-DYING IN PERU

On a farm between the rainforest
and the highlands, a grasshopper is dying.
It is night and he is surrounded by gringos.
We think it's a good idea to set it free,
drop it from the second floor of our home.
It jumps out the window as we try to hold it, flash
lights from cameras in its flickering eyes.

We've learned the sunlight in the rainy season
is finicky, too—cloud-gripped and squashed.
Rain washes coffee plants unstable. We think
we're drowning, too, in the hued landscape
of our new home—we, the young gringos
in rubber-slick waders, fertilizing plants
hanging on the mountain's slippery edge.

TO THE BABY TOAD WHO LUNGED UNDER MY ROLLER SKATES AT ADA HAYDEN PARK

I mistook you / for a cricket / for a stone / for a small / hole in the pavement / your dark body only / a shadow until I saw / your long legs stretch out / you airborne / then flattened / I admit that I've been there too / mistaken / for something else / deflated / under someone else's momentum / I bounced into it / when I meant to jump out / I know some / that are luckier / maybe your brothers / a man / that dresses like a boy / who sometimes likes me / leaves / his keys in the ignition / his car unlocked / my poppy did too / once / none of these men believe / that anyone would steal / from them / what a privilege it is / to believe / that no one will / steal / your way out / but I don't know / if these acts / are accidents / or intentional bravery / and when I die / I don't imagine / others will know either / what I mean is I too haven't loved / life / not precisely enough / to lunge away from the oncoming / danger. Maybe I love / it too much / I shift / for the sake of momentum / not seeing the wheel / trying not to think / about what someone could consume / if this body is my own / to have / if this body is still a body at all / or the left / key / in the ignition / now I always look down / at my feet / looking for life / in dark places / in damaged concrete / mulberry stains / hoping I won't hurt / another / the leather of my skates / the red and green flag of you / remind me our mutual miscalculations / clumsiness / when trying to step out / someone else's way / we anticipate the air / the unbalanced / swerve or hop / the place we land when it's over / and they've passed safely / we never imagine / the possible / the pressure / our own end.

FORGETTING, SPEECH

I am talking   the children are   watching
the bat fly   around the ceiling   they think
it's a bird   I remember   my lover wedged
between two trees   trying to push himself up
in cowboy boots   he tells me not to
help the children tell each other HIT IT HIT IT
HIT THE BIRD   the bat flies faster   in circles
away from its nest in the rafters   placed
next to the ball the children kicked   last week
the bat settles makes no sound   the children
forget go back to the games   he is quiet
at night our bodies touching   I've grown
accustomed to our half-truths   I love hymns
when his voice sings them   the way his hips
move to rhythms   the way he spends most
mornings whistling instead of talking I will not
let myself love him   but I do love   the kids
they tell me we will have a good day they won't
waste milk or water in their fruit   or cornbread
saturating it like they did yesterday   they never

want directions   just space   to make mistakes
to ruin   what they think   won't hurt them
to destroy   I overhear one ask   what to do
if the adult   watching them drowns   they are
told to call for help   they forget   their coats
when they go home   it's hot then   distracted
by the bat   I forget my keys, too   my fears
why does it have   to end   sleep is a waste
of breath   I close my lips   to rest   to watch
the hips   the hymns the hums   the time   the ball
the bat drop from the wall   wings open this time

TO THE GNAT WHO FLEW INTO MY MOUTH

I opened   it to yawn didn't mean   to engulf you my therapist
asks the difference   between always and never   I tell her
they both measure something infinite   like water our house
the ocean mom's   grandparents crossed   *can you clarify*
she asks   *you're my dancing girl* mom sang   every night
I didn't dance   they are adverbs   I say we are all
adverbs   she takes notes   she doesn't know me
yet   doesn't know one day   it was always   winter Mom
didn't let the fire exhale   drunk didn't open the flue talked
about new   wooden logs that smolder emerald   seafoam
every other decoration only blue or brown   wallpaper ship
anchors hanging frames   her smiling   face wearing white
on a dock   she never stopped   missing   the boat the sun's
fever   the nautical life   she no longer lived   now
landlocked with two   children   in her first
home   I won't go back   my therapist goes on
vacation   there's no medicine   that makes mom's house
a sail   docked   no bars   of her guitar   birds
sing   in her grave she is still   in her murderer's
                    basement I am   the attic

—where did you think you were going?

There's no way out, not the mouth.

Not the teeth.

Not even the dung.

RECOGNIZING BOOKS IN ITALIAN AT A NEW LOVER'S APARTMENT

Sometimes what's familiar can't be
read, only seen. Sometimes the picture
tells the whole story. Sometimes it doesn't
matter if it does.

> I can say good-bye

in every tongue native to my friends.
In Portuguese, I say *beijos*. In French,
I remember only *il neige*. In German,
entschuldigung or *guten tag*. Mostly, I say
sorry. Sometimes for things I haven't done.
Sometimes my body betrays me. Sometimes
his does instead.

> There are days I let the water

run too long. There are days I just want
to be wet or warm, instead of cold, tired.
There are days where above is a mirror
for below. Where the blue of the sky

is the blue of the flame. There are days
where the body
             is the only word or phrase.

POEM WITH ENTITLEMENT

The crawfish guard the trail, clawing
at my wheels every time I get close.
I don't know what drew them
from the water, angry at anyone near.
I've been here before, too. Blaming
others, snapping when someone neared.
Like they dried up my home, forced me
to roam the jagged
concrete with the others
who've been displaced—now lonely
and small like me. I am still
not always able to see beyond
my own body, to reach toward
the shore instead of those who've walked by
unknowingly or those who've reached out
only trying to pick me up. I am never
sure what is destined to hurt me.

MANIC PIXIE DRUNK GIRL

Her mood is a genie in a snowglobe.
Her look is a snow woman with a button
nose, jeweled lips, and 80's hair.
Some days, all the hands shaking
the glass drop glitter in her strands.
Sometimes they shake the perfect messy bun.
In the purse hanging off her branching arms,
anything you might want: a flask, cigarettes,
aspirin, marshmallows, chocolate,
ready for any bonfire, ailment or thirst.
She can make you smile, boy, even hung
over. All of her tears are tears of joy.
Her nipples are warm coals in the February
snow. She can open the closed
sex shop to make sure you get the love
you want. She only defeats you in bed, where
she chokes the right part of your neck,
bites your ear lobes with pop rock sparks.
Her limbs are monkey bars and you're

always welcome. Don't shatter
the glass, darling. Let your eyes
accumulate the snow.

THE HOUSE PLANT

after Sabrina Orah Mark

SOME THOUGHT it was because of all the men I wasn't fucking. Others thought it the men I was. Still, a friend said it might do me good, make me less lonely. By then, I had wet dreams of masturbating alone. I didn't want to talk to anyone. I ate sandwiches under the desk and they called me by name on the loud speaker. I didn't breathe. The mouse jumped out of a box of books. The kids chased it into the woods. These woods' kids had no mothers, just leaves. Perhaps cicada murmur. Leaping toad fingers. I was lost in the forest tapestry. My white walls had nail teeth that bit the print still. I named the morning hush *Not Baby, But Something that Needs Care,* and then *Poverty, or the Outsides of Poets* and finally *If Drunkenness Were Closer to God.* One night I thought I made it out, but it was only under. I stripped my clothes unlike a newborn. But like kudzu vines. Like something I saw when I walked too far. Hanging in effigy of the swamp. Maybe the past. Back then, we hopped the pool fence and jumped in with the vacuum snake. It wasn't the snake that made us turn, but what walked in the corner, before cameras, by the trash cans and beach chairs and concession stand and lights, with dark stone eyes. They were all there, rolled up, ready to be fed. At home, there was a new still I didn't yet name. With aloe arms. I thought, *Here Could Be Where She Doesn't Light*. I knew that it would die. Every day closer to my blood like tired miners sleeping on the job.

SELF PORTRAIT WITH A LIT CIGARETTE

A chipmunk made his home
under the front step. I shaved
my legs with a rusty razor
and made corn beef hash
for breakfast. My brother is getting
married. My sister is finally
home. Here I am alone
wondering if the chipmunk
prefers Bach or Tchaikovsky,
why skin can't rust, if sex
is ever worth love, which trees
the chipmunks stole the walnuts
from. I am not disillusioned.
I know they do not need me.
But I kept trash bags by the opening
before I knew he was there. Always
burying life beneath everything
we've wasted. So many holes closed
up. So much we throw away.

TO THE MAN WHO LEFT THE SAUVIGNON BLANC IN MY FRIDGE

I drank it all
looking out
the window
searching for everything
I didn't find in you.
It tasted green & dry.
There is never enough
time. I love
in apologetic odes,
which is to say
I never love at all.

MY PHONE: A TOMBSTONE
MEMORIALIZING

failed dates—mostly men
I don't remember, men I haven't wanted.
My best friend says I'm lucky
to be where I am. Today,
drinking chamomile vodka
with grapefruit. I try not to hate
myself for minutes at a time.
I haven't written a poem in two weeks
and no one's asked. What would break
my parents' hearts more: admitting I'm bi,
or disowning God? My house is empty.
I'm tired of being fat. Autocorrect changes
"cried" to "fried." I dream every night
about women. The gossiping winds
won't hush. The ants colonize
the carpet. I read the morning paper.
The bees survived the burning church.

POEM WITH AVOIDANT-BORDERLINE
PERSONALITY DISORDER

Every text starts like a poem
that stops at send. There is a man
with an abominable snowman hat
in the hallway shouting. A poet says
every story has a word and I get
younger and younger, shrinking.
The first time the therapist told me,
Of course you love your mother.
I never went back. Of course I didn't.
The first time I heard a bone break
it sounded like the roller rink.
Like landing wheels and a woman's
shrill scream. But it wasn't mine.
That early chaos. That early ending.
I don't know what it feels like to care
for anything without losing
the night. The cat who let himself in
was not a stray. The woman in heels
limps because one of them is broken.

It's been years since I've worn any.
I hang red pumps next to a forest
tapestry, pretend stillness counts as art.

AGAINST MARRIAGE

I thought garlic lasted forever
until I saw the brown holes in its side,

the green sprouting from the top.
Nothing stays young. I've melted

so many plastic containers in the microwave
because they couldn't take the heat.

The only jewelry mom wore without
green gems were her wedding rings

that turn my fingers green
now that she's gone. I find a bar

where I like to read books. I leave
when the bartender falls in love with me.

I find a new coffee shop with lemonade.
I'm allergic to caffeine. The maple trees

tint my house red in the dying
colors of the day. Will I live longer

alone, or with someone else? Love
is not a safe space and it's hard

to tell the difference
between privilege and optimism,

branches of the same tree. The worst
way to eat yogurt is with a fork

even though that's the best way
to eat the crepe that holds it. All

the voices of the white men eating breakfast
beside me sound the same, like someone I knew.

A woman says her husband can't hear
women's voices. That's why

he never understands her, can't listen,
says it's worse on the phone.

ROLLER RINK

If I am driving too slow
        you are probably driving too fast, 93,

the year I was born.
        I stopped asking questions the day

he left. Now it's Friday
        and the roller rink is open.

I hold the door, hold the sweaty glass
        of water after fast laps,

hold the hands of a blonde four-year-old girl.
        She looks like she is tripping

but never falls, always reaches out
        when she sees me swing by

she smiles. When I sit down, she tells me
        she will be there for eleven more hours.

It's not true. The five-year-old nearby tells me
      to race—the men race each other

I race home instead.
      I am unwilling to try anymore.

When I was younger, we picked up
      games of street hockey on rollerblades.

Now, I stand hip-to-hip beside girls who hold me
      up, bruise me sometimes.

I bruise myself, too, with hits I choose to give
      but there are rules in derby that everyone follows.

There are penalties, there is dust
      on the track. We go in circles.

Does god or death last longer?
      I am unsure. The music says god

is strength—bigger than men
      who tell me they love me

so I will let them play. I eat
      skin. I, too, am hungry

in the drought
      of summer wind and sun.

SHOWER HAIR EKPHRASIS

It looks feminine on the ceramic tiles.
The hair, swirled into the shape of a small face
with curled locks hanging down
beside what appears to be an enlarged belly.
Head bowed, praying. When asked to describe me,
the pastor said only "searching." I have trouble
letting go. Would you rather
a damaged baby or an empty lawn? Grass
breathes and love, too, has always been
so biblical. Would you rather a virgin mom
or the truth? A woman tells me
my widow's peak is beautiful and rare.
The man I fuck lets his dog stay in the bed
when we do it. At dinner, he eats the whole lime—
even the rind. I just want to feel safe. The water
roads maps on my back, peoples murals
from my fallen hair. I have my own place,
but I don't know the distance
between beauty and time.

TO THE FLOWERS I DROWNED LAST YEAR

on my birthday: you're not the only beautiful thing
I've lost to smothering. I've always believed more was

best: more money, miles, sunsets, and rises.
Although you're dried now, brittle from the last time

you had enough nutrients to weep, I still touch you
sometimes, sun you enough that I can tell the roses

from the leaves, lilies, and carnations—to remind me
how bright your colors could've been if I had

given you time to drink what was offered, digest it.
If I had waited until you asked for more.

PENNIES

Rumor has it Lincoln was a tenor,
but the copper has no sound. I kick

pennies the color of your beard
on evening walks. You said, "Write me

a poem," I sipped some wine. "You might be
the funniest person I've ever met."

But I look down when I walk. That's how
I find the pennies that I hide

under my pillow where I placed teeth
when I was younger. I stopped

believing in the tooth fairy when I found
the keepsake necklace in mom's drawer

next to the panties, rum, and note
in her cursive. I still believe in God

some days, because I find pennies
and nickels when I walk to the lunchroom,

just enough to buy a small snack.
Sometimes a full lunch. They say

Lincoln always told the truth.
It made him boring, too,

always knowing what to expect.
But that's not the case with you,

not yet. Only sound, the raspy
gaze of gentle lashes, soft

words in earth tones, dry eyes
in nights still absent of floral moons.

VALENTINE'S DAY

When my grandmother asks me,
wine drunk, *Did you get anything good
from me?* she means my nails. Gone
three years to the day now, my nails
chip no matter how much I file them,
no matter how low they're cut. My hair, too.
My jacket smells like PBR and American Spirits.
My bed smells like the two-year-old used
condoms pressed between my sheets and the box
spring. My living room smells like August meets
a receding skyline in the blues of a guitar
riff. I never wrote love poems until I loved
a man more than myself and I had to
reimagine heart in the inner child
of every poem, in the electric
hangover of a sunny Saturday. Every time
a heart breaks, God turns off
the ability to comment or share. Prayers
are penny stocks in a volatile market

that say only *I had one pleasure
I could spare,* or *I'm giving away
another rusted copper hope.*

SELF PORTRAIT WITH YESTERDAY'S MAKEUP

I skate the smudged

    concrete

        beside the rhinestoned

            curls

       of the water's blue hair.

I am waiting

    for the feelings to dry.

       Don't

worry: it takes years to evaporate

          ghosts.

      Soon it'll be another

lamped

    evening, in the quiet

         pillow

of my favorite books.

            I take

    notes.   Autocorrect changes

"femininity"

    to "felinity." I want to turn

      all

m's to *l*'s and half the *n*'s,

                              but I have

never been thorough.
                         The youngest
adults speak only

                         in hashtags.
                    Autocorrect changes "nerds"
                    to "beers."
                                   Thank god
          for computers cleaning up
  our words.

                         Thank god for poet
eyes
          to crimp the fragile

                                   mood.
  I make wishes on my eyelashes that fall

                    down
the parched soil

                         of my cheek's
dry skin

II.

One day, the urge to write a poem became bigger
than the urge to write a suicide note.

— BLYTHE BAIRD

THE PRIEST READS THE LINEAGE OF JOSEPH
ON CHRISTMAS DAY,

instead of the story about Mary's conception,
or Jesus' birth. *But I'm Catholic,* my friend
tells me. *I don't read the Bible. It was so strange.*
Over drinks, our horoscopes tell us to start
an elaborate rumor about ourselves
and see how far it goes. We laugh.
All of our boyfriends are moving out.
The sky blares through the blinds: a neon
OPEN sign. Like the white taillights
on the car in front of me that made me think
I was driving the wrong direction: there are
always distractions. Open skies, lights
directing you into on-going traffic. *Stay*
in your lane, an older woman told me
every day I created something new.
Stay, a man told me when I looked away
at every loving touch. *Sink,* says
my clearance bed, *into the last five years,*
a hollow print angel in the worn fabric.

DAYS OF 2000

I was never good at swimming / like the rest of my family. That year, / I wore swimmies to keep / my head and shoulders above / the edge. I protected / my barbies / the way I protected / myself, but my brother still / managed to pull their heads off / and I still managed / to tie their hair into knots / when I meant to untangle it / and isn't that how life is, / more knots / when we mean to untangle / my hands are strands / more often / than they are combs / When I told him / I didn't think I could love / anyone else / this way again / I meant / that loving him felt like / that day / in 2000 when my lungs / emerged as chlorine waters / I had already gotten out / of the pool / grabbed a carrot / from the garden / decided to go in / but when my brother threw / my barbie in the water / I didn't notice my arms were bare / I jumped / and the water was the foggy horizon / of my last sunset / My dad's face turning red / *you could've died* / *what were you thinking?* / Not about myself / what I mean is sometimes / we are so focused / on someone else / we don't notice / we stepped into something / we might not come back from / I don't like pools / for the same reason / I don't like love / they are stronger than my body / the thoughts swim right / out of my head / now I live in a place / so windy / the water at the fountain / blows right out of my mouth / and this, too, feels like a kind / of drowning / gasping for something you need / but can't have

MERRYMEAD FARM

At the end of August, pumpkin seedlings dug
deeper into the earth, got ready to stretch—roots
like arms, hands, feet running—through cornfields.
Every time I got lost, tried to blow on pieces of corn

stalk, but only dad learned how to make grasses
whistle. When I finally escaped the maze, I'd eat
ice cream. Hug dad. Watch the leaves change.
Pet the cows. Pray for mom again. Hope that this year,

September would remind me of simple pleasures:
the slick surface of a muddy soccer ball, grass
stains on my fragile knees, encouraging talk
on the sidelines that kept me fighting to stay alive.

But every year while I would play, the pumpkin seeds grew
larger, sprouted. I waited until October to rip them
from their roots, empty them of their bellies,
carve shapes or faces in their ragged skins.

SELF PORTRAIT, SKEPTICAL

Do the clouds remember a time
they were ice on the surface, blotches

of some body of water? Do they miss
the way people looked up, saw

truer their faces? Do they still carry
the weight of the bodies that plunged,

felt the ice's melting surface heavy, hard
and didn't wake? Do they forgive

themselves for dissolving, then ascending
toward the sun? Do they shimmer,

despite their heights, for the sadnesses
still? Is sadness singular? Are clouds?

Is the sun's hot breath a mother's
love, a comfort spread across

the sky, a foaming crown in the blue?
Is the water in the lake buried alive?

If my body were a sky, would I see
my breath, the wind an invisible fog?

When I finally grey,
will I get to choose where I fall?

48 HOURS

In September, we walked
through the woods we thought
would give us a view, but opened
to a clearing instead.
We held hands and jumped
under an autumn waterfall
into water shallower than us.
Later, our bodies rejected
each other: after going too deep
my dinner in chunks
on his skin. His leg
seizing every time he fell
into sleep, waking beside
a stranger he shared too many
secrets with. A discomfort
in silence and connection.
Empty kisses. Hands only
holding onto hope, but not
this. Mine a body used

to being alone. His still
remembering someone else.

SELF PORTRAIT DATING MID-20S

I see my reflection on the sidewalk
as I walk to my car—the face of a fox
in a puddle of its melted body.
And then again in the electrical lines
as I drive to work—all tilted
after recent storms. There was a time
I stood taller—freshly-built muscles
I sculpted, hair I straightened to match
expectations. I've grown bored of it all
& deflated: a balloon. Though superficially
loved, so easily and naturally let go. I've let
all my balloons go, too, to places
I've never aspired to reach. When I look
behind, autocorrect changes "back"
to "Bach." Think of something else
instead, it urges, but when I get home,
the water in the toilet won't stop flushing.
I've still loved one man the whole time
I've desperately tried to love someone else.

TO THE SERPENTINE BELT THAT FELL OUT
THE BOTTOM OF MY CAR IN THREADS

your split / was preventable / I thought the leaking / engine
wouldn't matter / if I replenished it / once emptied / I was wrong /
it ravaged more than just you / other parts nearby / that couldn't /
handle the constant / grease / and how many times / has
something broken / because I didn't fix / what I knew was wrong /
but who am I / to apologize / for what I've done / as if this is the
first time / I am the reason / for the threading / when I was
younger I sewed / fabric into purses / dresses / what I mean is
there was a time / my hands were thimbles instead of needles / I
unraveled threads only / to fashion something new / more vast /
that could be worn / in the sunflower field / an autumn hayride /
the pumpkin patch / by the scarecrow / I never knew / if those
dresses frayed / or fringed / I was too proud to ask / I left them /
for the comfort / of my own room / if I were a mirror / the
problems would be larger / than they appear / no, if I were a
mirror / I wouldn't reflect back at all / what I mean is I had hope /
if I could conceive / beauty / wholeness / self-reliance / I would
lighten / lilac / even in moonlight / but knowing others deserve
better / doesn't make me better / the whole body still flammable /
words choking / knowledge / insufficient to heal

POEM WITH AVOIDANT-BORDERLINE
PERSONALITY DISORDER II

I chased a chipmunk from church
on Sunday. The door was left open.

The kids let it in while they threw rocks
by the playground. I stopped

for a dog on the side of the road,
but the car coming towards me

didn't. The owner scooped up
its limp body, head dangling,

blood trailing. Men have come close
to falling on me. Once at Mardi Gras

from a balcony on Bourbon Street.
Another through the frame

of a restaurant. The last time
someone fell on me, it was a woman

and I still couldn't catch her.
I watched the man from Bourbon St.

walk three blocks on a broken
tibia, one cop on each arm.

The chipmunk left the church before
the kids got the chance to touch it.

I watched the news for weeks, but
never discovered what became of him.

INDIGO SNAKE

Flying above Atlanta at night
the ground looks like black sky

with constellations below:
instead of Sirius, the whale

that swallowed Noah, or was it
Jonah? I'm only religious in love

with anything. I find myself
studying long hours. I want

to be an expert. I observe you
sleeping—hold my breath, pretend

my heartbeat stops so I can feel
yours. Outside, the silver hair of the clouds

wait for old age. A man once told me
the indigo snake wouldn't hurt

herself trying to swallow you.
Even if I could, I wouldn't grow old

with you. I made a mistake—I only
open locks with keys made for doors.

Windows are curtains between you
and we, but I say no again and again

to myself. I talk too much to hold the indigo
snake calm in my arms in the darkness.

SELF PORTRAIT WITH SMALL TOWN WEEKEND

There are times no one wants
to pot succulents with me. After two
beers, I accidentally insult my friend's
wife when I mean to give her
a compliment. The bartender tells us
she is moving to the countryside,
won't eat any more peaches.
I eat tomato soup with moldy basil
for breakfast because don't we all want
more green? Every time I open
a can, I eat the label, too. I wouldn't survive
winter without the socks my ex bought
me the Christmas I was supposed to meet
his new lover. There is tea
in the cupboard, my new diffusers.
I don't have good feelings for anyone
I love. My aunt tells me to carry a weapon.
Look how far it goes, she smiles
as the hornet spray erases what is

unseen in the yard. We are used
to idea of danger. There are no glasses
that completely block out the sun, no facial
that can heal the moon's cratered face.

POEM WITH ABANDONMENT ISSUES

"Like any artist without an art form, she became dangerous."

— TONI MORRISON, *SULA*

The kid at the beach digs a hole
to trap the water. He thinks he can
make it stay. People always leave
for the reasons they originally fall
in love. Toni Morrison died today.
I try to fill the absence—hands
with flour, mouth with biscuits.
The sunflowers attract flies. I write
poems about something I can't touch.
The dog chases rabbits
and squirrels in the backyard
for hours. I am my mother every time
I am lonely. I'd rather be

the other woman than be with any man.
Everyone I want to love
loves someone else or goes. Like death,
so active, hobbied, abled.

OBSERVING SILENCE AT THE BAHA'I HOUSE OF WORSHIP, WILMETTE, IL

At night, even the crickets are hushed.
From the garden, wind carries the scent
of ringed flowers and sounds of steadfast
fountains. Only half-drawn, the moon hangs
over trees, ornamental. The pillars seem
woven with lace. I read a sign by the door:

No photography. Observe silence.

I stand in the back. Two women sit silently
in the front. The temple is as quiet as it had been
in Frankfurt. I remember arriving there too early
for the Feast of 'Izzat. But the temple had been
empty—under construction. Strangers prayed
in German outside. In Illinois now,

I begin searching for a prayer in the book,
but the only section for women ends
with one man. A signature—*Bahà'ullàh.*

I wonder: *Did they ever notice the women
are missing?* I start to speak, but I realized
the others left. From my seat in the temple, behind
stiff curtains and lace, so did the veil-sheer moon.

TO THE APPLE LEFT FERMENTING IN MY CAR

I don't know how I forgot

                     about you—pink lady

with cheeks plump as my own.

                 It's my biggest fear, too,

that I will grow softer,

                 decompose and no one will

notice.

         I'm good at goodbyes.

                  My first boyfriend and I

never ate

         apples together or talked

                   about much.

My second boyfriend ate

                  apples in the shower

after a trip to the orchard.

                 I threw my third boyfriend

into the shower.

                 He had so many

fleas. Now he showers on his own—

                   wears button-ups,

styles his hair like a grown man.

           My last

boyfriend took cold showers,

           didn't like to be wet

or naked.

         I'm less

           vulnerable than I used to be,

—my hair the humid ripeness,

             sticky skin.

I'm surprised the time

           alone has bruised you

only slightly.

           Your color preserved.

TO THE CHILD WHO PUT ROCKS ON HER TONGUE

Your hands are still dirty, don't lick
them: there are wipes that will cleanse
your skin before you taste the past
hour you spent on the gravel. No,
the wipe won't taste any better
than your arm—a bed of sweat drops
and dust at the local drive-in. I know
you're skeptical. I, too, have questioned gifts
given by strangers. I've placed rocks
on my tongue, smiled with pebble teeth.
I didn't expect it them to taste so much like dry air,
frosted pine needles, grainy metallic earth lint.
After so much time touching other things,
my hands stopped tasting like me. I tried
as you did, to rid my tongue of everything
I hadn't ever meant to swallow.

HARMONS, JAMAICA

You took the coconut from my hands,
teaching me to open up. The knife cut
the coconut's skin. It smelled like summer
and the meat peeled easily like my sun-burnt
skin—in strips of white, slimy and thin
like tongues. We drank the cloudy water
as ash from the burning
garbage fell on our cheeks. Days later,
passing by the sugar cane fields,
I still remember the sweetness.
My palms sweat. My fingers still sticky.

KAYAKING IN OKATOMA, MS

The drive was orchestral music and cannons.
But the overture doesn't stay *alla marcia,*

it flags like the oars we took turns rowing
along slow currents. We gave each other time

for food, bug spray, being eaten and melted.
My skin birth red with brown spots. His skin

golden, a prize I could touch. We raced away
from the others so we'd find our own space:

a kiss beneath the lazy branch we'd discover
when we paused, the shirt he left behind

like memory. How long have I settled
for a love that only rests? With no sprints, give

or takes, clumsy breaks on a sandy embankment?
Let me be the water without jutting branches, hold

our boat steady and store the bursting of cannons
in my wet pockets long after our song has ended.

POEM WITH PTSD

I was operating on a blind unicorn
in my dream. I was a doctor, up all night
trying to make her see. I grew tired.
The nurses brought me food,
but the pizza was a puzzle that couldn't be
eaten. When I awoke, I thought
it was real: the aggressive legs
of the unicorn, the hunger, the desire.
To be told what beats you isn't even
there. To be consumed, solving
problems for just a taste
of what others freely enjoy. To be born
in the middle of someone else's suffering.
To lead blind fantasy to healing.

SELF PORTRAIT IN THE INSECTARIUM

Grief is a supervised visit
to the butterfly wing with no

flap or voice. It lingers:
protocol. All the butterflies

in the unsupervised place
are dead threaded with pins

that make them look alive,
only resting in less green.

Do you notice the insects
are dying? Polar vortex, they say.

Magnetic north is shifting,
they say, unlike wings.

My heart is beating properly.
I cannot caterpillar

on the tree to change.
Even if I could, I would

wake in a glass room, low
ceiling. There would be snow,

and sun so close. Glossy
light, warmth out of reach.

"BUT YOU WERE SO CLOSE!"
—THEY ALWAYS TELL ME—

to accomplishing the whole task of anything:
a career, a 150 lb squat, a plowstop
on my skates, a mastered scale, a boyfriend.
That's how I orgasm, too—I don't. I stop
before I get there. That's why I'll never be
a suicide. I prepare everything and then quit.
Weight loss, too. One week in and I drink
a whole bottle of wine and devour a pizza.
No abs. No insta fame. I come close to everything
I want to touch. Not Icarus—I don't get
burned—I stop flapping my wings, pass out.

I FALL IN LOVE WITH THE GHOST OF MY PAST SELF

in every new relationship. There she is:
crying in bed. *There! There!* says the exit.

It's so sad to see you get in your own way,
says her work. *Leave the roadkill behind,*

I tell her as she tries to carry it. *You never
knew that animal,* I say as she packs

fallen leaves and fresh apples
into a small box instead. *I want to*

send him the fall, she explains.
When it comes in the mail, he keeps

it in his closet. Around her, the tree's
leaves ember to brown, her eyes

gradually molten. *I saved the best
ones for you,* she smiles, remembering.

She imagined he enjoyed the skin
between his teeth, the sweet juice. *They were*

real? He asked stunned, holding
the rotted season in his house.

AT THE ULTRASOUND

The woman with her hand inside me
says I ask good questions. I want to
know how it works. She says
the probe records vibrations—the sounds
form a picture. *Could our words*
change the look of my organs?
She says only if she were closer
to my neck. I don't believe her.
Maybe that's why everything inside
looked unremarkable. How strange
that technology hears our pain
into pictures, that talking can affect us
less from a distance, even when
another sound has a hand inside us.
After the appointment, I heard learning
through the back of the blackboard,
another teacher in an adjacent room.
When the results came, she found no
cysts or stones, just visible ovaries,
a functional bladder and uterus.

LEARNING TO TRUST MY INSTINCTS

If you can't have luck with one thing you
*   try another*

— BUKOWSKI

I read *You Get So Alone at Times It Just Makes Sense* on the PATH train from Hoboken to Manhattan. F. was four blocks from my stop, shopping with his sister on Broadway. I told him, *hurry.* I hadn't seen him in more than a year, but I had a long day and we lived close enough: him in the Bronx with his family; me with my boyfriend north of the city.

I hated walking in Times Square, through the tourist streets, where I tried to always look down, listening only for danger, or poems. I wore a cotton dress with Grand Canyon tones, strapless, and sandals of starless galaxies.

I never saw him look at me that way—reserved. In college, we talked freely about Professor Michaels' fear of aging, the way he cried during *Amour,* the way we all did. We'd debate the ethical dilemmas that *Hable Con Ella* posed and shared what we'd been reading. He always had a movie list ready.

Oh, that's just the way he is, his sister told me. But I was right, it'd be years before we'd talk again. He'd be working as a bank teller in the Bronx and I'd be teaching in Jackson. He'd send me *Borges Collected Fictions* and *Between the World and Me,* apologize about the years. *You'll marry the next man you date,* he told me with confidence.

But I'd bring the books with me to every city. Heartbreak stays on every shelf unread.

MY FRIEND TELLS ME LOVE ISN'T FINITE

which is why he can kiss me and still
have plenty left for his wife. I get it

in theory, but it's not what I want.
When another friend asks, *do bats*

even like the houses boy scouts are
building for them, I think, should we be

building at all? In the TSA line, there are
Christmas songs sung by agents

in three languages. I notice everyday
juxtapositions: on different corners of one

warehouse: a law firm & an insurance
company; a church & a furniture store.

I eat three meals at once, read poems
to my therapist afraid my problems

bore her. *Stubborn child! Delete*
that stanza, a friend says after too many

nights of me ignoring everyone's advice:
I can't help it. These words feel like

all I have. I cry every time I listen
so I avoid the news. The radio says *old*

age is happier. We stop making new
old friends. My date doesn't understand

why this makes my eyes well—he's still in love
with his ex, lives in his hometown—

his family and his high school friends
around him. I never thought people would

grow if planted, but I'm learning.
We only leave so we don't have to change.

Dad always said, *when you go, you take*
yourself with you. I know I don't

have a choice, but to heal
or to go and still I know which one I'll always

choose. In every bar, a mirror
of who I've been before. In every

coffee shop, a familiar mug.

SELF-PORTRAIT WITH MILEY CYRUS

I built the wrecking ball in the dream.
She rode it. Then, I used it on my favorite
restaurant. Soon, songs. Then memory.
Everything swings. The horsetail grass
looks like an ashing cigar. Beside me
the tree roots are not deep enough to be more
than a horizon. I sit. Nothing is blooming—
the tint on my car is orange dirt the storm
brought in from Odessa, not pollen. I still
sneeze. Maybe it reached Miley, too.
Maybe it didn't. I go to church on Sunday
to babysit, not to pray. Last week, a girl
said her dog was trained not to run away,
but when he grew up, he forgot a lot.
The children, too. A mother told me winter
was long enough that her son didn't recognize
the dickcissel's songs. He thought it was
an alarm. From my window, the sound
of the wind, swallows, and cars are church

bells in e-minor. When I open my eyes,
the mountain hangs a rainbow in front of its body,
like a dress rarely worn, but casually admired.

A LOVE STORY, OR NOT

He thinks he likes Bukowski. That's what he's reading. *Notes from a dirty old man*, sitting next to what he thinks is a pretty flower, Queen Anne's Lace. He takes a break to run. Though the tops are more yellow than he remembered, he doesn't think it matters. No one told him about the wild parsnips, what they could do when touched. But he learns when the sun comes out and his skin is no longer his, but the brown apple that poisoned some princess in a story that his sister or him is supposed to love, but neither did. And a woman's kiss, from some eve, from some body of water, from some daybreak, never saves a man in those stories, even though maybe they both wish it would. There's no shade. His new lover's body is a dress that she's afraid will fit another's body better. Or maybe belongs on a thrift store shelf. Maybe nowhere at all. The Bukowski book is gone, and all that's left is Carson McCullers' *The Heart is a Lonely Hunter*. But the heart isn't lonely, it's just in the appendix and doesn't quite do what it should. The new lover's mouth could be a wild parsnip, too. It could be nothing. It could be all tongue and teeth.

SELF PORTRAIT AFTER POLAR VORTEX

Around me, the sound is the rapid
melt of snow, not falling rain.
The blind dog on the trail looks
in my direction. The runner does not.
The purple martin only sees his body
in patches of lake ice. There's still
snow. I measure the cold in pairs

of socks I need to wear to keep
walking. How did the purple martin
survive three days without running
water? It's beginning to flow
again. On the bank, people line up
like geese. Love is dangerously
thin. Go ahead. Fish on the ice.

TRIPTYCH ON A SERVICE TRIP TO CRANKS CREEK, KY

I.

That day, the sun was wedged between the trees.
We hammered nails into sheets of plywood,
built walls around an empty frame. By supper,
we needed to rest. After working, we hiked
the mountain to kill time. It was hard, you know:
the walk. Before us, a sharp incline. A boulder
balancing on a precipice. Pebbles or dead branches
dropping with our steps. And yet the woman
we were helping, the one with cancer, wanted
to climb to the top with us. We left her behind.
That night, my dreams were white and skeletal;
Kentucky a valley of dry bones. I spoke in my sleep
to a chill bunk. They slept through it, as did I.

II.

Charlene has no teeth I can see. When we look
away, she places a cigarette between two gums.
Her toilet is an ashtray. I talk to her when I have
free moments. She tells me she will die soon.
Her cat drops hair on the kitchen table, but
we make sandwiches there anyway. She asks
for ham and cheese, opens a Coke. Everyone
seasons her floor with mud on our lunch hour.
On our laps, the cat does not purr, like he knows
we are foreign: we are galactic debris, space junk,
her house a black hole. I've never been more
afraid of absence. The space heater snaps the way
the animals won't. Charlene is quiet, too, but we
are chatty today after our work and don't notice.

III.

The day we left, my hair got caught in the fingers
of the tree. They asked us to stay. We promised
summer, but knew that summer might not come.
Earlier that week, I started to cry when they spoke
of our privileges and Charlene as an inspiration.
We don't even know her. Once we leave, how
will the smoke dress her children? Powder her carpet?
Here we did nothing but build a roof, walls, hammer
the floor. We want to think we made a difference.
And we did. In a few months, she will move into a new
home. Forget the crooked walls, the cinder block
foundation. Forget the rushed hammering, unleveled
doors. Ignore her bad habits. The cancer. The past
abuse of her child. The poverty of her years.

ACCEPTANCE

The moon is a dull eye.
The sky is a prosthetic
blue. I didn't ask to be

in the room reflective of its light,
the phantom limb of the day.
Maybe I'm already dead. Beside

me the prairie grass is stale
bread flaking in the wind. I do not
ask for second chances. The sun

is not patient, but shy.
When morning comes, flushed
with clouds, I do not ask it

to stay. The bees don't
seek pollen from brunette
clovers. The beekeeper doesn't name

all the bees. The way things end
always change our understanding
of the journey. The birds sing

their favorite tunes every day,
forgiving. Maybe one day
I'll sing, too.

ON THE SHORTEST DAY OF THE YEAR

She told me she could teach me
to relax. We settled into bed, stripped

down to our words. Before the sun fell,
somewhere a man rode a bicycle

on a lake I hadn't yet known. In the middle,
at the thinnest part of the ice. My therapist asks,

why do you feel guilty? He didn't drown.
In bed, she lifted the covers, her lips

a slit sun on a blush horizon. No blue
light blaze bothering our eyes—

awash. Somewhere outside her room,
someone burned a Confederate flag

and it looked like America. Not our quiet
night, where she taught me to care

for myself despite the dimming of outside
flames. The soft glow, the accumulating ash.

POEM FOR MARY

The train comes more often at night.
I didn't know this until I was sober at 12 am

on a Sunday crying. The sound didn't soothe me
the way it normally does. I took a walk

through the fog that fell. One night, we went skinny
dipping in the pool at the top of Gilbertsville Road.

There were no cameras back then—just stadium lights,
slow moving water, pool chairs. A skunk came by the edge

of the water. You told me to relax. You were the first woman
I ever kissed. I knew you couldn't stand me, you wanted

to touch me because my body looked the way you wanted yours to.
You drew an anarchy symbol on your wrist when you wanted

to feel rebellious. I ate strawberries before dinner
without my dad's permission, let you sneak through my back door

to meet your parents at the front when the boy that raped you
wanted to hang out. The woman I love like a mother loved you more.

I was always jealous of you for that, for your mind,
for your sense of humor, the way you could sing. I was

lead soprano before you came to my school. I took a backseat for
you. It hurt you that your dad was in love with me.

I've never felt loved, you know. The last time I saw you,
you shouted the n-word on South Street, left me

in two feet of snow at 4 am beside men that looked
twice our age. I took a train to see you. I realized I wouldn't

marry him. I ran to the past. You told me we'd see a ballet.
I never have. It doesn't matter now. I wish I had the courage

to stay silent or to lie like you do by myself. Instead, I drink whiskey
tea and pray that god exists somewhere in the walls

beside the cockroaches, beetles, larvae, dust, wood—

APPROACHING ANOTHER UNREMARKABLE
SEASON

Only some of the painted ladies
rise from the gravel road.
In the slow wind, my hair
is a cloud. My skin—
summer heat. When I ask
for what I need, I become
wherever I am, fragments
of butterflies beside the car
wheels, trapped inside the grill.
On one side, a severed
antennae, a quartered wing.
I have no choice, planted—
a small tree by the algae-floral lake.
There are leaf hoppers trying
to make a home in my toes,
sweat bees on my skin's bark.

NEW BEGINNINGS HAIBUN

He has four laughs, but one is silent. I have only three and all of
them are loud. I used one the first time we kissed. The sound was
American, the way I say his name. He doesn't mind. Sometimes
he even tells me it's cute. I stuck a quail egg inside my body today
because loving him makes me itchy. He doesn't notice if he feels
that way, too—it's not his insides that burn. Lucky him. The cells
in my cervix are precancerous. My chances of getting cancer are
higher if I smoke. My doctor tells me, even just one cigarette. I tell
her don't worry, but it's hard to write poems when you're falling
in love. I use an adverb every time I imagine his smile. Like I need
it *very much*. Like anyone *certainly* cares about the details, regards
the description of even small motions. Instead of "kill two birds
with one stone," some insist, "feed two birds with one scone." But
I have no interest in nesting. Even though it is winter. We
hyphenate our lips, not our names. We see stories we already
want to tell, not the sun or the trees. When we look up,

   the clouds are cursive
    letters. Love is snow, I sled
    in the debris.

SUNDAY

When Hanif writes, "loneliness is a type
of debt," I wonder *to whom?* There was a year

I dreamed every night I died
in a tsunami, as if the ocean was close

enough to render fear, as if I loved it
enough that I would let it

swallow me. But if I tell you dreams are
a kind of prayer, if I tell you sometimes

I'm awake when I sleep, I mean these words
are a canary warning what awaits. I've never studied

enough to become fluent in another tongue.
Most days my tongue sits against the roof

of my mouth, not proctoring
words, never checking the answers. I know

the work of a poet is not to love,
but to encounter it. What I'm saying is

that *debt* is another word for *duty*
and loneliness feels more like a tax

for reaching inward, separating waves
or wave lengths into only words. On paper,

I'm only one color. Loneliness is not
a rainbow, but a wandering strand.

On the last day, god said it was good.
And then the week started over again.

SELF PORTRAIT WITH RUM AND COKE, LOOKING BACK

This time three years ago, I was brown bagging a beer by Mayes Lake reading Reginald Dwayne Betts' *Bastards of the Reagan Era*. Last week I called the suicide hotline and they asked if I could call a friend. Back then, I didn't have any friends nearby, just a notebook. I went to crawfish boils with strangers where we smelled honeysuckle vodka from the distillery during the humid afternoon, our hands cajun-spiced as we sucked sweetness from the heads we opened. The music's rhythm threw off our own. When I finally settled down, I ate delta tamales in the pickup truck of a man I loved but knew I would leave. He was happy there. He didn't mind the improvisation of jazz, the lonely highways, the small talk everyone used to avoid the weight we all felt as the heat sat heavy on our skins. *At the end of life, a secret,* Betts wrote. But there was no secret I kept, not for myself or others. I modeled in a contemporary exhibit at the Mississippi Museum of Art, stood as the living form of the artist's imagination. Men took pictures with my naked, painted body. I stood cold and bored in heels, bowlegged, waiting for the spectacle to end. Men now tell me I'm too big for them, I have a mustache, will I change? *I just wish you were more tidy.* They mean my greying eyelash hair, my obscene poetry. I've exchanged beer for clearer liquors. I've exchanged lakes, men.

NOTES

The opening line of "Take it From a Rufous-Collared Sparrow" was inspired by the opening line of "We Manage Most When We Manage Small" in *All of It Singing: New and Selected Poems*

"To the Woman Who Feels No Pain Due to a Genetic Mutation" is written to Jo Cameron, the woman discussed in the BBC Scotland online news journal on March 28, 2019. The story was covered by Claire Diamond. According to the article, Jo never needed a painkiller—not even during childbirth. Although she wouldn't change her life, "she thinks pain is important."

"The House Plant" was inspired by Sarah Orah Mark's poem "The Babies."

The structure of "Sunday" was modeled after Hanif Abdurraqib-Willis' poem "A Poem in Which I Name the Birds." The quote comes from his poem "Love Your Niggas" in his collection *A Fortune for Your Disaster*.

ACKNOWLEDGMENTS

Thanks to the editors of the following journals in which these poems originally appeared, often in earlier forms:

- "Self Portrait in the Insectarium," The Threepenny Review
- "Self Portrait after Polar Vortex," The Hopkins Review
- *"Self Portrait in a Thunderstorm," SWIMM*
- *"To the Woman Who Said I Was 'Too Normal' For Therapy," and "To the Baby Toad Who Lunged Under my Roller Skates at Ada Hayden Park," Anomaly Literary Journal*
- "To the Woman Who Said I Was 'Too Normal' for Therapy,"

  Poetry Daily (re-print)
- "Take It from A Rufous-Collared Sparrow," *Drunk Monkeys*
- "Grasshopper-Dying in Peru," *Coldnoon*
- "Sunday," *After the Pause*
- "Days of 2000," *Driftwood Press*
- "New Beginnings Haibun," *Pidgeonholes*
- "A Love Story, Or Not," *Goliad Review*
- "To Gnat Who Flew Into My Mouth," *Storm of Blue Press*
- "Self Portrait with a Lit Cigarette," and "Poem with Avoidant-

  Borderline Personality Disorder," *honey & lime*

- "Against Sentimentality," *Salamander*
- "Kayaking in Okatoma, MS," *Eunoia Review*
- "Self Portrait, Skeptical," *Firsthand Poetry Anthology*
- "Observing Silence at the Baha'i House of Worship, Wilmette, IL," Green Blotter
- "Portrait of the Alcoholic's Daughter," *Ghost City Review*
- "Forgetting, Speech," "Poem with Depression," and "The

  House Plant," *Royal Rose Review*
- "Self Portrait Dating Mid-20s," *Thimble Literary Magazine*
- "Against Marriage," (originally as "At Lockwood Café") *Revo-lute Magazine*
- "Poem for Mary," Telephone Booth Project in Council Bluffs, IA
- "My Phone: A Tombstone Memorializing" in *Pirene's Foun-tain: A Journal of Poetry*
- "The Priest Reads the Lineage of Joseph on Christmas Day" in Lyrical Iowa

Gratitude to so many beautiful people who inspired this collection: from those that broke my heart to the friends that loved me so well it taught me how to love myself. You've all inspired my growth as a person and poet: Donna Spruijt-Metz, Brittany McLean, Dana Bridges, Jessica Luke, Jenny Marsh, Patience Young, Freddy La Force, Caleb Rainey, Aline Prata, Kevin Scott Marken, Ashley Bleicher, Eileen Forsyth, Allison Durazzi, and Tori Miller. I love you all so much.

Thanks to my family for supporting me and loving me from afar for so many years. I appreciate how you supported to me, even when you didn't share my love or interest in art. It means a lot.

Thank you to Iowa State University for the time and financial resources to develop this collection. Special thanks to my close friends Debra Marquart, Kate Wright, Keygan Sands, Kartika Budhwar, Richard Frailing, Alana Jones, Chloe Clark, Caroliena Cabada, Hagan Whiteleather, Zach Lisabeth, Nancy Hayes, Allison Justus, Julia Bilek, Ana McCracken, and Amalie Kwass-man-Sage for the brilliant insights, craft talks, and meals or drinks together on bad days. Your support and kindness is a poetry to me.

I'm indebted to the work of writers I've fallen in love with: Debora Kuan, Diannely Antigua, Shelley Wong, Rena Medow, Hanif Abdurraqib-Willis, Paige Lewis, Catherine Barnett, Kaveh Akbar, Shira Erlichman, Charlotte Seley, Victoria Chang, Adam Zagajew-ski, Jericho Brown, Diane Seuss, Michael Mlekoday, Sabrina Orah Marks, Lisel Mueller, Lucille Clifton, Ocean Vuong, Mei-Mei Berssenbrugge, Jack Gilbert, Linda Gregg, and many, many more. You're a gift and I hope all of my readers explore your poetry, too.

ABOUT THE AUTHOR

Crystal Stone is an east coast girl with a Philly attitude. She is the author of four poetry collections *Knock-Off Monarch* (Dawn Valley 2018), *All the Places I Wish I Died* (CLASH 2021), *Gym Bras* (Really Serious Literature 2021), and *Civic Duty*, forthcoming from Vegetarian Alcoholic Press (2022). Her work has previously appeared in *The Threepenny Review, The Hopkins Review, Writers Resist, Salamander, Poetry Daily* and many others. She is an MFA graduate from Iowa State University, where she gave a TEDx talk called "The Transformative Power of Poetry" in April 2018.

You can find her at her website www.crystalbstone.com.

ALSO BY CLASH BOOKS

BURIALS
Jessica Drake-Thomas

HELENA
Claire L. Smith

REGRET OR SOMETHING MORE ANIMAL
Heather Bell

I'M FROM NOWHERE
Lindsay Lerman

HEXIS
Charlene Elsby

BURN FORTUNE
Brandi Homan

CENOTE CITY
Monique Quintana

LIFE OF THE PARTY
Tea Hacic

PAPI DOESN'T LOVE ME NO MORE
Anna Suarez

CL4SH

WE PUT THE LIT IN LITERARY

CLASHBOOKS.COM

FOLLOW US

TWITTER, IG, FACEBOOK

@clashbooks